SIMPLE STEPS TO BUILD GOOD HABITS AND BREAK BAD ONES

By

Eric Patterson, PhD

Table of Contents

Chapter 1

Understanding The Psychology Of Habits And How They Form

Have you ever found yourself reaching for a snack without even thinking about it, or automatically checking your phone as soon as you wake up in the morning? These are examples of habits, and they play a significant role in our daily lives.

But what exactly is a habit, and how do they form? According to psychological research, a habit is a behavioral pattern that has become automatic and unconscious through repetition. In other words, habits are actions that we do without consciously thinking about them.

Habits are formed through a process called habit formation, which involves three stages: *the cue, the routine, and the reward.*

The cue is the trigger that initiates the habit. It can be a specific time, place, or activity that prompts the habit. For example, the cue for a habit of checking your phone first thing in the morning might be the sound of your alarm clock.

The routine is the actual habit itself. In the example of checking your phone, the routine would be picking up your phone and scrolling through social media or checking your emails.

Finally, the reward is the positive outcome that reinforces the habit. In the phone example, the reward might be the satisfaction of staying connected with friends and family or the sense of accomplishment from completing tasks on your to-do list.

By understanding the psychology of habits and how they form, we can begin to identify our bad habits and start developing strategies for building new, more positive ones.

Here are a few practical tips for getting started:

Identify your cues: Pay attention to the times, places, and activities that trigger your bad habits. This will help you understand what prompts them and allow you to develop strategies for avoiding or changing these cues.

Experiment with rewards: Try using different rewards to see what works best for you. For example, if you're trying to build a habit of exercising regularly, you might reward yourself with a healthy snack or a relaxing activity after each workout.

Seek accountability: Share your habit-building goals with a friend or family member, and ask them to hold you accountable and offer support and encouragement.

Be patient and persistent: Building new habits take time, and it's normal to encounter setbacks along the way. Don't get discouraged, and keep working towards your goals.

Chapter 2

Identifying Your Bad Habits And The Triggers That Lead to Them

In order to break bad habits and build good ones, it's important to first identify what those habits are and the triggers that lead to them. This process of self-reflection and evaluation can be challenging, but it's an essential step in the habit-change process.

One way to identify your bad habits is to keep a habit journal. In this journal, you can write down the habits you want to change, the triggers that lead to those habits, and your thoughts and feelings around those habits.

For example, if you're trying to break the habit of procrastination, you might write down:

1. Habit: Procrastinating on work tasks
2. Trigger: Feeling overwhelmed or anxious about the task
3. Thoughts and feelings: I don't know where to start, I'm afraid I won't do it well, I'll do it later when I'm in the mood

By identifying the triggers that lead to your bad habits, you can begin to understand the underlying causes of those habits and develop strategies for addressing them.

Here are a few practical tips for identifying your bad habits and the triggers that lead to them:

Pay attention to your thoughts and emotions: When you engage in a bad habit, what are you thinking and feeling at that moment? These thoughts and emotions can be clues to the underlying causes of the habit.

Experiment with different strategies: Try different approaches to changing your bad habits, such as replacing the habit with a new activity, setting clear goals and deadlines, or finding ways to reduce or eliminate the trigger.

Seek support: Talk to a therapist or trusted friend or family member about your bad habits and the triggers that lead to them. They can provide valuable insights and offer support and encouragement as you work to change your habits.

Remember, the process of identifying and changing bad habits is a journey, and it's important to be patient and persistent. With time and effort, you can develop new, more positive habits and break free from the negative patterns that hold you back.

Chapter 3

Setting Clear And Specific Goals For Building New Habits

Setting clear and specific goals is an essential step in building new habits. Without clear goals, it can be difficult to stay motivated and on track, and you may find yourself drifting away from your desired behavior. On the other hand, setting specific and achievable goals can help you focus your efforts, track your progress, and stay motivated as you work to establish new habits.

Here are some tips for setting clear and specific goals for building new habits:

Identify your overall goal. What do you want to achieve through this new habit? Make sure your goal is specific, measurable, achievable, relevant, and time-bound (SMART). For example, instead of setting a goal to "exercise more," try setting a goal to "exercise for 30 minutes at least three times per week."

Break your goal down into smaller, more manageable steps. Instead of trying to change your entire routine at once, break your goal down into smaller, more achievable steps. For example, if your goal is to start meditating every day, you might start by meditating for just five minutes a day and gradually increasing the length of your meditation sessions over time.

Set a specific time and place for your new habit. Make it easier to stick to your new habit by setting a specific time and place for it. For example, if your goal is to start reading for 30 minutes before bed, make sure you have a designated spot in your home where you can curl up with a good book.

Track your progress. Use a habit tracker or journal to keep track of your progress and celebrate your small victories along the way. Seeing your progress can be a powerful motivator and help you stay on track.

Find an accountability partner. Having someone to hold you accountable can be a great way to stay motivated and on track. Find a friend or family member who can support you in your efforts to build new habits.

By following these tips and setting clear and specific goals, you can increase your chances of success in building new habits. Remember to be patient with yourself, as it can take time to establish new habits. With persistence and determination, you can achieve your goals and create lasting change in your life.

Chapter 4

Making A Plan For Replacing Bad Habits With Good Ones

Are you tired of feeling guilty about your bad habits? Are you ready to make a change and improve your overall well-being and happiness? Making a plan for replacing bad habits with good ones is a crucial step in the process of self-improvement. Here are some strategies and practical examples to help you get started.

First, it's important to identify the root cause of your bad habits. Are you bored, stressed, or seeking comfort or distraction from something else? Understanding the motivations behind your habits can help you come up with more effective strategies for change.

Next, it's time to set specific, achievable goals. Instead of simply saying you want to "eat healthier," try setting a goal to eat three servings of fruits and vegetables per day. This makes it easier to track your progress and hold yourself accountable.

To help you stick to your new habits, it's also helpful to have a support system in place. Surround yourself with people who encourage and motivate you, and consider finding a mentor or accountability partner to help you stay on track.

One practical strategy for replacing bad habits with good ones is to create a trigger and reward system. For example, if you want to start exercising more, make a pact with yourself to go to the gym every time you watch an hour of TV. As a reward, treat yourself to something you enjoy, like a healthy smoothie or a new workout outfit.

It's also important to be patient and understanding with yourself. Change doesn't happen overnight, and it's normal to have setbacks along the way. Remember that progress, not perfection, is the goal.

So if you're ready to make a change and replace your bad habits with good ones, start by setting specific goals, finding a support system, and using triggers and rewards to help you stay on track. With a little planning and perseverance, you can break free from those bad habits and create a happier, healthier life for yourself.

Chapter 5

Building New Habits Through Consistency And Repetition

Building new habits can be a challenging task, but it is an essential part of personal and professional growth. One key to success is consistency and repetition. By consistently performing a new behavior over time and repeating it regularly, you can establish it as a habit and make it a part of your daily routine.

Here are some strategies and practical examples to help you build new habits through consistency and repetition:

Start small: It's easier to build a habit if you start with small, manageable goals. For example, if you want to start exercising regularly, start by committing to just 10 minutes of exercise each day. Once you've established this habit, you can gradually increase the duration of your workouts.

Set a specific time and place: Choose a specific time and place to perform your new behavior each day. This will help you create a consistent routine and make it easier to remember to do the behavior. For example, if you want to start meditating, set aside 10 minutes each day at the same time and in the same place to practice.

Use a reminder or trigger: A reminder or trigger can help you remember to perform your new behavior. You can use a physical reminder, such as a sticky note on your bathroom mirror, or a digital reminder, such as a phone notification. You can also use a current habit as a trigger for your new behavior. For example, if you want to start flossing your teeth every night, you could set a reminder to do it after you brush your teeth.

Seek accountability: Having someone hold you accountable can be a powerful motivator. Consider enlisting the help of a friend, family member, or coach to help you stay on track with your new habit.

Celebrate your progress: Don't forget to celebrate your progress and give yourself credit for the effort you put into building your new habit. Whether it's a small reward or a simple acknowledgement of your accomplishment, recognizing your achievements will help you stay motivated and on track.

By following these strategies and consistently repeating your new behavior over time, you can successfully build new habits and make them a part of your daily routine. Remember to be patient with yourself and give yourself time to adjust to your new habits. Building a new habit takes time and effort, but it is worth it in the end.

Chapter 6

Using Rewards And Incentives To Motivate Yourself

Rewards and incentives can be powerful motivators, especially when it comes to self-improvement and personal goals. Whether you're working towards a big project at work, trying to get in shape, or just trying to be more productive in general, rewards and incentives can help you stay motivated and on track.

One of the key strategies for using rewards and incentives to motivate yourself is setting specific, measurable goals. By setting clear, achievable goals, you'll have something to work towards and a way to measure your progress. You can then use rewards or incentives to help you stay focused and motivated as you work towards your goals.

For example, if you're trying to get in shape, you might set a goal to run a certain distance in a certain time frame. Once you achieve that goal, you could reward yourself with a new running shirt or a pair of shoes. Or, if you're working on a big project at work, you might set a goal to complete a certain number of tasks in a certain amount of time. Once you reach that goal, you could reward yourself with a day off or a night out with friends.

Another strategy for using rewards and incentives to motivate yourself is to track your progress and celebrate your achievements. This can be as simple as keeping a journal or using a planner to mark off tasks as you complete them. Seeing the progress you've made can be a powerful motivator and help you stay focused and on track. You can also celebrate your achievements by rewarding yourself with something special, like a day at the spa or a trip to your favorite restaurant.

Finally, it's important to be realistic when setting goals and rewards for yourself. Don't set the bar too high or you might become discouraged, and be sure to choose rewards that are meaningful and motivating to you. Remember, the key is to find what works best for you and stick with it.

So next time you're feeling unmotivated or struggling to stay on track, try using rewards and incentives to help you stay focused and motivated. Whether you're working towards a big project at work, trying to get in shape, or just looking to be more productive in general, rewards and incentives can be powerful tool for self-motivation.

Chapter 7

Finding Accountability And Support From Others

Accountability and support from others can be incredibly valuable in helping us achieve our goals and reach our full potential. Whether we're working to improve our physical health, advance in our careers, or simply make positive changes in our lives, having someone to hold us accountable and offer encouragement can make all the difference.

So how can we find this accountability and support? Here are a few strategies and practical examples:

Join a group or community that shares your goals. Whether it's a fitness group, a professional association, or a hobby club, being part of a group of like-minded individuals can provide the accountability and support you need. For example, if you're trying to lose weight, joining a weight loss support group can provide motivation and accountability through regular weigh-ins and progress check-ins.

Work with a coach or mentor. A coach or mentor can provide one-on-one accountability and support as you work towards your goals. They can help you stay on track, offer guidance and advice, and provide encouragement when you need it most.

Make a public commitment. Sharing your goals and progress with others can provide added accountability. Consider starting a blog or social media account to document your journey, or tell your friends and family about your goals and ask them to check in with you regularly to see how you're doing.

Find an accountability partner. Partnering with someone who is also working towards similar goals can provide mutual accountability and support. You can hold each other accountable and encourage each other to stay on track.

Ultimately, the key to finding accountability and support from others is to be open and vulnerable about your goals and struggles. By seeking out the help and encouragement of others, you can create a powerful network of support that will help you achieve your dreams.

Chapter 8

Overcoming Common Challenges And Setbacks In Habit Change

Habit change can be a difficult and often frustrating process. We all have habits that we want to change, whether it's eating healthier, exercising more, or cutting back on our screen time. However, it can be tough to stick to our goals and make lasting changes. Here are some common challenges and setbacks in habit change, and strategies for overcoming them.

One common challenge is a lack of motivation. It's easy to start a new habit with enthusiasm, but it can be difficult to keep up the momentum when the initial excitement wears off. To overcome this, try setting small, achievable goals and rewarding yourself for meeting them. For example, if your goal is to start exercising regularly, set a goal to work out three times a week for the first month. When you reach that goal, treat yourself to something you enjoy, like a new workout outfit or a massage. This helps to keep you motivated and on track.

Another common challenge is a lack of time. Many of us lead busy lives, and it can be tough to find time to fit in new habits. To overcome this, try prioritizing your habits and making them a priority in your schedule.

For example, if your goal is to eat healthier, plan your meals in advance and prepare healthy snacks to have on hand when you're on the go. This helps to ensure that you have healthy options available when you're short on time.

Setbacks are also a common challenge when it comes to habit change. It's easy to slip up and revert back to old habits when we're feeling stressed or overwhelmed. To overcome this, try to anticipate potential setbacks and have a plan in place to deal with them. For example, if you're trying to cut back on your screen time, make a list of other activities you can do when you're tempted to spend too much time on your phone or computer. This could include going for a walk, spending time with friends or family, or taking up a new hobby.

Ultimately, habit change is a process, and it's normal to face challenges and setbacks along the way. The key is to stay motivated, be proactive, and have a plan in place to overcome these challenges. With time and practice, you can create lasting habit changes and live a healthier, happier life.

Chapter 9

Using Visualization And Visualization Techniques To Stay On Track

Visualization is a powerful tool that can help us stay on track and achieve our goals. By creating mental images of our desired outcomes and the steps needed to get there, we can increase motivation, focus, and clarity. In this article, we'll explore some strategies and practical examples for using visualization and visualization techniques to stay on track.

One effective strategy for using visualization to stay on track is to create a vision board. A vision board is a collage of images, quotes, and other motivational items that represent your goals and aspirations. To create a vision board, gather images and words that represent your goals and arrange them on a board or paper. Place the board in a location where you'll see it often, such as on your desk or in your bedroom. Seeing your vision board regularly will help you stay focused and motivated to achieve your goals.

Another visualization technique that can help you stay on track is visualization meditation. This involves closing your eyes and picturing yourself achieving your goals. Imagine the sights, sounds, and feelings you would experience if you were already living your desired outcome. This can help you stay motivated and focused on your goals, as well as increase your belief in your ability to achieve them.

One practical example of using visualization to stay on track is to visualize your daily routine. Before you go to bed each night, take a few minutes to visualize your next day. Imagine yourself waking up on time, eating a healthy breakfast, and completing all of your tasks efficiently. Seeing yourself successfully navigate your day in your mind can help you stay on track and make better decisions the next day.

Another practical example is to use visualization to visualize your long-term goals. If you have a big project or goal you're working towards, take some time to visualize yourself completing it. Imagine the steps you'll take, the challenges you'll face, and how you'll overcome them. This can help you stay focused and motivated as you work towards your goal.

In conclusion, visualization and visualization techniques can be powerful tools for staying on track and achieving our goals. Whether it's creating a vision board, practicing visualization meditation, or visualizing your daily routine or long-term goals, these strategies can help us stay motivated, focused, and on track. So, it is always a good idea to incorporate visualization into your daily routine.

Chapter 10

Incorporating Mindfulness And Self-awareness Into Your Habit Building Journey

Incorporating mindfulness and self-awareness into your habit building journey can be a game-changer for achieving your goals and living a more fulfilling life. These practices allow you to tap into your inner wisdom, cultivate a deeper understanding of yourself, and make conscious choices that align with your values and priorities.

Here are some strategies and practical examples for incorporating mindfulness

and self-awareness into your habit building journey:

Set aside dedicated time for mindfulness and self-reflection: This could be as simple as taking a few minutes each day to sit in silence and focus on your breath, or setting aside a longer block of time for journaling or meditation. The key is to make these practices a regular part of your routine, rather than an afterthought.

Practice non-judgmental observation: When building new habits, it's easy to get caught up in a cycle of self-judgment and criticism. Instead, try to cultivate a sense of curiosity and non-judgmental observation. When you catch yourself engaging in negative self-talk, try to take a step back and observe your thoughts and feelings without judgment.

Seek out opportunities for self-discovery: Engage in activities that allow you to explore your strengths, values, and passions. This could be through personal development courses, workshops, or simply taking time to reflect on what truly matters to you.

Seek support from trusted sources: Building new habits can be challenging, and it's important to have a support system in place to help you stay on track. This could be a coach, mentor, or a group of like-minded individuals who are also committed to personal growth.

Be kind to yourself: Remember that building new habits takes time, and it's normal to have setbacks along the way. Be kind to yourself and recognize that progress is a journey, not a destination.

By incorporating mindfulness and self-awareness into your habit building journey, you'll be better equipped to navigate the ups and downs of change and create lasting habits that align with your values and goals.

Chapter 11

Using Technology And Tools To Help You Build And Maintain Good Habits

Building and maintaining good habits can be a challenging task, but with the right tools and technology, it can become much easier. By using technology and tools, you can track your progress, set reminders, and hold yourself accountable to your goals. Here are some strategies and practical examples for using technology and tools to help you build and maintain good habits.

Use a habit tracker app: Habit tracking apps allow you to set goals, track your progress, and see how long you've been able to maintain your habits. Some popular apps include Habitica, Loop, and Streaks. These apps can help you stay on track and motivated by showing you your progress over time.

Set reminders on your phone or computer: If you struggle to remember to do certain tasks, setting reminders can be a great way to stay on track. You can use the built-in calendar or task list on your phone or computer, or use a reminder app like Remember the Milk or Todoist.

Use accountability tools: Holding yourself accountable to your goals can be difficult, especially if you don't have a support system in place. There are several tools that can help you stay accountable, such as Beeminder, which allows you to set goals and track your progress, and Stridekick, which turns your fitness goals into a friendly competition with friends.

Take advantage of social media: Social media can be a great way to stay motivated and on track with your habits. You can join groups or communities dedicated to your goals, or use platforms like Instagram to share your progress and get support from others.

By using these strategies and tools, you can make building and maintaining good habits much easier and more enjoyable. With the right technology and tools, you can track your progress, stay motivated, and hold yourself accountable to your goals, ultimately leading to a happier, healthier lifestyle.

Chapter 12

Finding Balance And Avoiding The Pitfalls Of Perfectionism

Perfectionism can be a double-edged sword. On one hand, it can drive us to succeed and strive for excellence in our personal and professional lives. On the other hand, it can also lead to unhealthy habits and a constant feeling of inadequacy. Striving for perfection can lead to unrealistic expectations, a constant need for approval, and an inability to enjoy the present moment. It's important to find balance and avoid the pitfalls of perfectionism to live a healthy and fulfilling life.

So, how can we find balance and avoid the negative effects of perfectionism? Here are some strategies and practical examples:

Set achievable goals: Perfectionists often set unrealistic goals for themselves, leading to constant disappointment and frustration. Instead, try setting smaller, achievable goals that you can accomplish. This will give you a sense of accomplishment and keep you motivated to continue working towards your larger goals.

Practice self-compassion: Perfectionists are often their own worst critics. Practice self-compassion by acknowledging that you are human and will make mistakes. Instead of beating yourself up, try to be kind and understanding towards yourself.

Learn to accept imperfection: It's important to remember that perfection doesn't exist. Accept that things will not always go as planned and that it's okay. Embrace your imperfections and focus on what you can control.

Seek support: It's okay to ask for help and seek support from friends, family, or a therapist. It's important to have a support system to help you through tough times and remind you that you are not alone.

Take breaks and prioritize self-care:
Perfectionists often push themselves to the
limit, leading to burnout and exhaustion.
Remember to take breaks and prioritize self-
care. Whether it's taking a walk, getting a
massage, or simply taking some time to
relax, make sure to take care of yourself.

By following these strategies and
incorporating them into your daily life, you
can find balance and avoid the pitfalls of
perfectionism. Remember that it's okay to
strive for excellence, but it's important to be
kind to yourself and embrace imperfection.

Chapter 13

Using Positive Affirmations And Self-talk To Boost Your Motivation And Confidence

Using positive affirmations and self-talk to boost your motivation and confidence can be an incredibly powerful tool in helping you achieve your goals and reach your full potential. By repeating positive statements to yourself, you can improve your mindset, attitude, and outlook on life, ultimately leading to increased motivation and confidence.

One effective strategy for using positive affirmations and self-talk is to create a daily affirmation routine. This could involve setting aside a few minutes each day to repeat positive affirmations to yourself, either out loud or in your head. Alternatively, you could write your affirmations down and post them somewhere visible, such as on your bedroom wall or on the fridge.

Some examples of positive affirmations that can help boost your motivation and confidence include:

"I am capable and worthy of achieving my goals."

"I am confident and capable in my abilities."

"I am worthy of love and respect."

"I am worthy of success and abundance."

"I am strong and capable of overcoming any challenges that come my way."

Another strategy for using positive affirmations and self-talk is to focus on specific areas where you want to improve. For example, if you struggle with confidence in public speaking, you could repeat affirmations such as "I am a confident and skilled public speaker" or "I am at ease and composed when speaking in front of others."

It's also important to be mindful of the language you use when speaking to yourself. Avoid using negative or self-deprecating language, and instead focus on using positive and empowering words. This includes avoiding phrases such as "I can't" or "I'm not good enough," and instead replacing them with more positive statements such as "I can do this" or "I am capable and competent."

Another practical tip for using positive affirmations and self-talk is to surround yourself with positive influences. This could include seeking out supportive friends and mentors, listening to inspiring podcasts or books, and surrounding yourself with positive imagery and quotes.

Ultimately, the key to using positive affirmations and self-talk effectively is to be consistent and persistent. It may take some time to see results, but by consistently repeating positive affirmations to yourself and surrounding yourself with positive influences, you can significantly boost your motivation and confidence over time.

Chapter 14

Getting Back On Track After A Relapse Or Setback

Relapses and setbacks can be difficult to deal with, especially if you have been making progress in your goals or recovery. It can be easy to feel discouraged and lose motivation, but it is important to remember that setbacks are a normal part of the journey. The key is to take a step back, reflect on what happened, and find ways to get back on track. Here are some tips for getting back on track after a relapse or setback:

Reflect on what happened: Take some time to think about what led to the relapse or setback. Was there a trigger that you weren't prepared for? Did you feel overwhelmed or stressed? Understanding the root cause of the setback can help you better prepare for similar situations in the future.

Don't beat yourself up: It is important to be kind to yourself and not dwell on the setback. Remember that setbacks are a normal part of the journey and everyone makes mistakes. Instead of dwelling on the past, focus on what you can do to move forward.

Seek support: Don't be afraid to reach out to friends, family, or a therapist for support. It can be helpful to talk through your feelings and get perspective from someone else.

Make a plan: Once you have reflected on what happened, it's time to make a plan to get back on track. This might involve setting new goals, creating a schedule, or finding new ways to cope with stress. Whatever it takes, make sure you have a clear plan in place to help you stay on track.

Seek accountability: It can be helpful to have someone hold you accountable for your goals. This might be a friend, family member, or a therapist. Having someone to check in with can help you stay on track and motivated.

Take it one day at a time: It's important to remember that progress is made one day at a time. Don't get overwhelmed by trying to do everything at once. Take it one day at a time and focus on making small, consistent progress.

By following these tips, you can get back on track after a relapse or setback. Remember to be kind to yourself, seek support, and take it one day at a time. With time and effort, you can get back on track and continue making progress towards your goals.

Chapter 15

Maintaining And Reinforcing Good Habits Over Time.

Maintaining and reinforcing good habits over time is essential for personal and professional growth. Good habits can improve our health, productivity, and overall quality of life. However, it can be challenging to maintain and reinforce good habits, especially when they require a lot of effort or when we face distractions and setbacks. Here are some practical tips for maintaining and reinforcing good habits over time:

Set specific and achievable goals: Setting specific and achievable goals can help you stay motivated and focused on maintaining and reinforcing your good habits. For example, if your goal is to exercise regularly, you could set a goal to walk 10,000 steps per day or to go to the gym three times a week.

Create a supportive environment: Surrounding yourself with supportive people and creating a positive and organized environment can make it easier to maintain and reinforce your good habits. For example, if you want to eat healthier, you could stock your kitchen with healthy foods and avoid keeping unhealthy snacks in the house.

Track your progress: Tracking your progress can help you see how far you've come and how much you've improved. You could use a journal, a spreadsheet, or a habit tracking app to keep track of your good habits and to see how you're doing.

Celebrate your successes: It's important to celebrate your successes, no matter how small they may be. This can help you stay motivated and keep your focus on maintaining and reinforcing your good habits.

Stay flexible: Don't be too hard on yourself if you slip up or face setbacks. It's natural to encounter challenges and obstacles when trying to maintain and reinforce good habits.

Instead of giving up, try to find ways to adapt and overcome those challenges.

By following these tips, you can increase your chances of maintaining and reinforcing good habits over time. Remember, it takes time and effort to form new habits and make them stick, but the benefits are well worth it. With perseverance and determination, you can create a healthy, productive, and fulfilling life by maintaining and reinforcing good habits.

Conclusion

Building good habits and breaking bad ones can be a challenging task, but it is an important part of personal growth and development. Here are some tips for building good habits and breaking bad ones:

Identify your goals: Before you can build good habits or break bad ones, it is important to identify what you want to achieve. What are your long-term goals, and what habits will help you achieve them?

Make a plan: Once you have identified your goals, it is important to create a plan for how you will achieve them. This may include setting specific, measurable, achievable, relevant, and time-bound (SMART) goals, as well as determining what steps you will take to reach those goals.

Start small: It can be overwhelming to try to change too many habits at once. Instead, focus on building one good habit at a time, and gradually add more as you become more comfortable with the new habits.

Find a trigger: It can be helpful to associate a new habit with an existing one, such as brushing your teeth after you brush them in the morning. This can help you remember to perform the new habit consistently.

Keep track of your progress: It can be motivating to see the progress you are making towards your goals. Consider keeping a journal or using a tracking app to monitor your progress and help you stay on track.

Get support: Building good habits and breaking bad ones can be easier with the support of others. Consider enlisting the help of friends, family, or a coach or mentor to help you stay motivated and accountable.

Be patient and persistent: Building good habits and breaking bad ones takes time, and it is important to be patient and persistent in your efforts. Don't be too hard on yourself if you slip up, but instead use it as an opportunity to learn and make adjustments to your plan.

In conclusion, building good habits and breaking bad ones requires a clear understanding of your goals, a well-thought-out plan, and patience and persistence. By starting small, finding a trigger, keeping track of your progress, and seeking support, you can make lasting changes to your habits and achieve your long-term goals.

www.ingramcontent.com/pod-product-compliance
Lightning Source LLC
Chambersburg PA
CBHW051652250726
48653CB00007B/2625